Peer Pressure
Deal with it
without losing your cool

Elaine Slavens • Illustrated by Ben Shannon

James Lorimer & Company Ltd., Publishers
Toronto

You're in the mall

with your friends and you show them the pair of jeans you've been saving up to buy.

One of your friends says, "You must be kidding! Those jeans are so out of style! Where have you been for the last year?" Everyone laughs, and you feel your face turning red with embarrassment. Even though you love the jeans, you put them back on the rack and shuffle off with your friends.

You've just caved in to peer pressure.

Making decisions on your own is hard enough, but when your friends try to "help" you, it can be even harder to know what to do. This help might feel like encouragement, or it might feel like pressure. Peer pressure is when people your age — your peers — try to get you to look or act a certain way.

It's is not always a bad thing.

Friends often introduce each other to cool new stuff – like a great band or a sport. But peer pressure can also lead to the wrong things – like hurting someone or trying drugs. It can make you feel like you're being forced to do something you don't want to do.

In this book, you'll learn more about peer pressure — what it is, how it can be both positive and negative, and strategies for dealing with it.

Whether you put pressure on your friends, or you feel as though peer pressure is changing the way you act and look, this book is for you.

Contents

Peer Pressure 101   4
The Insider   14
The Outsider   20
The Witness   26
More Help   32

Peer Pressure 101

Everyone wants to fit in, right?...

Who wouldn't want to be like everyone else? Well, lots of people, but that doesn't mean that wanting to be a part of a group is a bad thing. It can help you to do your best by

doing well in school

trying new activities

volunteering to help people

getting involved in social projects

joining groups or clubs

But think about this: what if the need to be part of the right crowd makes you do things you don't want to do, like

be very thin or very muscled?

dress in a sexy or trendy way?

smoke cigarettes, drink alcohol, or take drugs?

skip classes or cheat on tests in school?

be friends with only certain people?

make fun of or gossip about people?

break the law?

get intimate with someone when you don't want to?

So, it's up to you. Only you can decide in each situation whether peer pressure will affect you in a good or bad way.

Peer Pressure 101

Pressure comes from...

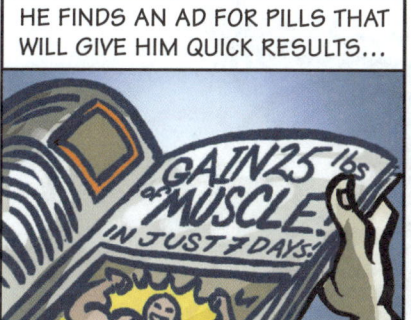

Peer Pressure 101

You know what they say: you gotta have friends. Your true friends don't pressure you to do stuff that makes you feel uncomfortable. And if you choose friends who feel the same as you about most things, it makes it easier to resist peer pressure from others. How do you rate as a friend? Check your score on the opposite page.

1 Can you be trusted to keep a secret and not talk behind a friend's back?
- ❑ rarely
- ❑ usually
- ❑ almost always

2 Do you let your friends make their own decisions, have their opinions, and disagree with you?
- ❑ rarely
- ❑ usually
- ❑ almost always

3 When a friend is really upset about a situation and says something mean to you, do you forgive them?
- ❑ rarely
- ❑ usually
- ❑ almost always

4 Have you ever done something nice for a friend even though it meant giving up something for yourself?
- ❑ rarely
- ❑ usually
- ❑ almost always

5 If a friend asks for your opinion, do you tell the truth instead of what you think that he/she wants to hear?
- ❑ rarely
- ❑ usually
- ❑ almost always

If a friend is going through a difficult time, are you able to stick by him/her even though you know that this will be hard to do? **6**
- ❏ rarely
- ❏ usually
- ❏ almost always

Do you let your friends talk about their problems when they are upset, even if you'd rather be talking about other things? **7**
- ❏ rarely
- ❏ usually
- ❏ almost always

If a very popular person starts paying attention to you, are you still loyal to your old friends? **8**
- ❏ rarely
- ❏ usually
- ❏ almost always

Are you able to compromise when you want to do something and your friends are in the mood to do something else? **9**
- ❏ rarely
- ❏ usually
- ❏ almost always

Can your friends depend on you to show up when you say you are going to meet at a particular time and place? **10**
- ❏ rarely
- ❏ usually
- ❏ almost always

Scoring

Each "rarely" scores 0.
Each "usually" scores 1.
Each "almost always" scores 2.

If you scored less than 10, you need to do a lot of work in the friendship department.

If you scored 10–15 points, you're a good friend, but deep down you probably know you could do better.

If you scored 16–20, congratulations! You're a great friend.

Peer Pressure 101

Dear Friendship Counsellor

Q: Why do people always talk about peer pressure like it's a negative thing? I don't think it's always bad. — *A Fabulous Friend*

A: You're right: peer pressure can be a positive thing. Your friends can help you to make good choices. For example, in some schools academic excellence is encouraged and that makes students strive to do their best. Peer pressure can also give you the confidence to learn a new skill that you otherwise would not have learned.

Q: All the kids in my group drink, smoke, and do drugs. I don't do these things but my friends keep wanting me to. What should I do? — *Under Pressure*

A: It's tough to resist this kind of peer pressure sometimes, but if you don't, you may face consequences that could last a lifetime. If you are feeling very pressured, then maybe it's time to find friends who respect your feelings.

Q: Do adults have to deal with peer pressure? — *Not sure*

A: Great question! Although it may seem that peer pressure is only a kid or teen issue, in fact, peer pressure happens to adults too. Many adults try to keep up with their neighbours — and with what TV and magazines tell them — by buying a certain car, sending their children to the "right" school, or dressing a certain way.

Q: I can't afford to buy the kinds of clothes the in-crowd wears, but I love the vintage fashions I've found at second-hand stores. People shouldn't judge you by how much money you spend on clothes, right? So why do they keep bugging me about the way I dress? — *Misjudged*

A: The in-crowd might feel threatened by anything outside their narrow vision of what is fashionable. If their teasing doesn't really bother you, then you are doing a great job of resisting their pressure on you to be a clone of them. But if what they say does bother you, it is important to tell them that you don't appreciate their comments.

| Peer Pressure 101 |

Putting on the
Pressure

Name-calling

"Hey, Slutty!"
Name-calling doesn't necessarily stop as you get older — it just gets nastier. It's often meant to make the person feel embarrassed enough to do whatever they can to put a stop to it.

OSTRACISM

"Hey, what are you doing here? This table is only for our group. Go eat somewhere else."
Some groups exclude outsiders, even if everyone in the group might not want to keep out others.

PUT-Downs

"I can't believe you're using that old cell phone. Where have you been? On another planet?"
Put-downs make people feel out of place, so they will do anything to avoid being humiliated in front of everybody.

DID YOU KNOW?

Research surveys have revealed...

- People feel much more secure about their beliefs and ideas

GUILT Games

"If you don't let me cheat off you, I'll fail this test."
Even good friends can make you feel that you are being disloyal to them if you don't do something that they want you to do.

Spreading Rumours

"Did you hear about Josie and Nick? Can you believe it?"
There's a reason you don't always know the source of a rumour: anonymity makes it easier for a crowd to target a person.

Physical HARASSMENT

"Let's teach this guy a lesson!"
Physical harassment is the most extreme way of forcing people to do something.

| when their peers seem to agree with them. | **60%** of Canadian teens think their parents are "very important." | **80%** think their friends are the "most important." | **2/3** of teens who have had sex wished they had waited longer. |

13

The Insider

You don't put pressure on others, do you?

Of course not! It's a free country, right? If you offer someone a smoke, they can say no. And you're being helpful when you point out that a friend is listening to lame music or wearing bad clothes. It's just a coincidence that all your friends look pretty much the same. Isn't it?

do's and don'ts

- ✓ Do try to recognize when you're putting pressure on others.
- ✓ Do ask yourself why you try to force others to do things your way.
- ✓ Do get help from a trusted adult if you're feeling out of control.
- ✓ Do learn strategies for dealing with people you are having difficulty with.

- ✓ Do try to make smart and safe decisions.
- ✓ Do think about the consequences of putting pressure on others.

- ✓ Do congratulate yourself when you treat others respectfully and kindly.

- ✓ Do think about how you would feel if someone tried to force you to do something that you didn't want to do.
- ✗ Don't get sucked into thinking that you can't change how you treat people. It may not be easy, but it is possible!
- ✗ Don't fight with others or threaten them to get what you want. It never works in the long run, and you end up losing their trust, respect, and friendship.

- ✗ Don't get involved in a group that puts pressure on others. Try to make new friends and treat them well.
- ✗ Don't solve your differences with people by acting aggressively. That never helps and only makes things worse.

The Insider

QUIZ

Friend or foe?

Supporting each other — that's what friendship is all about. But there's a fine line between encouraging someone and pressuring someone to do something. Take this quiz and see what you can find out. Of the following statements, how many are true, how many are false?

1. I have been called pushy.
2. When I get mad, I yell at people.
3. I fight with my family.
4. When people act a certain way, it bugs me.
5. When people disagree with me, I want to teach them a lesson.
6. When people don't want to do what I want, I get really upset with them.
7. There is a group of people that I can't stand.
8. I would never let someone get the better of me.
9. I have tried to get my friends involved in drugs or alcohol.
10. I belong to a gang.
11. I enjoy making fun of others.
12. I have sometimes intentionally left someone out.
13. I get into trouble at school.

I love to influence others.	14
I would never let someone make fun of me without getting even.	15
Dressing a certain way is very important to me.	16
I belong to an exclusive circle of friends.	17
There are many geeks and losers at my school.	18
I am tougher than others my age.	19
When a friend does something that I don't like, I yell at him/her.	20
It's important for me to act a certain way in front of my friends.	21
I am the leader of my group of friends.	22
I tend to boss others around.	23
I get into trouble with my friends.	24
I sometimes keep secrets from my friends.	25
There is a particular person that I can't stand.	26
When I meet this person I let him/her know how I feel.	27
I find it hard to control my anger.	28
I am not very tolerant of way people look or act.	29
Doing illegal things is exciting and fun.	30

Did you score a lot of Trues? Maybe it's time to start thinking about the way you treat people, and talk to someone about why you need your friends to do things your way.

The Insider

How to Stop Pressuring People

So you've thought about it and, sure, it's possible you can be a little bit pushy sometimes. Maybe even very pushy — a lot of the time! Knowing you treat people a certain way is the first step toward making a change for the better. The next time you feel the urge to push someone to do something they don't want to, try these strategies for backing off.

Take responsibility for the past. If you have already pressured someone, try to apologize and offer to make things better. Give them time to build up their trust in you again.

If you are tempted to get others to help you bend the rules, you might:

- Think about the consequences: getting into trouble; getting other people into trouble; making it hard for people to trust you, etc.

- Talk to yourself: "I am honest," "I don't want to hurt anyone," "It's not worth the trouble."

- Solve the problem. If you are tempted to cheat on tests, for example, admit you need the help up-front. Study with a friend next time or ask a teacher for help.

Learn how to control your anger towards people. Staying calm is a big part of making good choices. Some schools and community agencies offer courses designed to help you with this.

If you belong to a group that treats others badly, ask yourself if you really want to be a part of it. Are they really your friends? Friends treat others with respect and trust — do these people? Ask yourself why you are choosing to associate with only this group. Maybe there are other kids out there who are more like you.

Join a club that interests you. You will meet new people and learn new skills.

DID YOU KNOW?

10% of high school students suffer from an eating disorder.

80% of young smokers have a close friend who smokes.

Volunteer for work that interests you. It will bring out the positive side of you and make you feel good that you are helping others.

Give yourself a chance to learn new habits. Don't expect to be perfect all the time.

When Gangs are Involved

A gang is a group that gives its members a sense of belonging. You can often tell if someone is in a gang by a distinctive hairstyle, a dress code, or colours that they wear. Kids join gangs for many reasons: for friendship, to feel connected with others, to have something to do, for excitement, for protection, for money, or because they feel as though they have no choice whether or not to join. Unfortunately some gangs get involved in illegal activities. While it's true that it can be a good thing to be a part of a group, being involved in gangs could have serious long-term consequences, such as:

- Taking part in illegal activities such as theft, robbery, drug trafficking, extortion, threats, and violence
- Going to jail
- Hurting others
- Causing problems at home
- Getting hurt or killed
- Dropping out of school
- Making little money
- Closing off other more positive opportunities

It can be very difficult to resist joining a gang, but think about how much harder your life could be as part of one. The steps to avoiding a gang are the same as for other types of peer pressure:

- Stay calm, and understand clearly what you are being asked to do.
- Think about the consequences of joining.
- Think of an alternative.
- Explain why you don't want to join.

- **20%** of young non-smokers have a close friend who smokes.
- Study participants changed their quiz answers from correct to incorrect based on their peers' reactions.
- Kids who act out often seek their peers' attention.

The Outsider

Sometimes it's easy

to tell if you are being pressured, and other times it's not so obvious. Often the hardest thing is knowing people might make fun of you if you don't do what they want. You may go along with it but later regret it. Or you may go along with it without thinking about whether it is right or wrong.

Learn how to say no!
Here are some possible things to say get your point across:

- *"Let's do something else — I'm not into that stuff."*
- *"You see it your way, I see it my way."*
- *"If you are my friends, then back off."*

It can be hard to walk away from peer pressure, but it can be done.

do's and don'ts

✓ Do make a list of things that you can say when you are faced with pressure.

✓ Do try to ignore or avoid situations in which you will feel pressured.

✓ Do tell your parents or a teacher if you are in an uncomfortable situation with peers that you feel you can't get out of.

✓ Do realize that it's always your choice to make safe and wise decisions for yourself.

✓ Do try to learn assertive strategies to use with your peers.

✓ Do make a list of possible friends who can help you get out of an uncomfortable situation with peers.

✓ Do realize that you are not alone in your situation and can do something to get out of it.

✓ Do choose your friends wisely. If you want to stay clear of alcohol or drugs, choose friends who don't do alcohol or drugs. If you don't want to do illegal activities, choose friends who are law-abiding.

✗ Don't let your peers make you feel as though there is something necessarily wrong with being different.

✗ Don't blame yourself. You didn't do anything to deserve this.

✗ Don't try to deal with it on your own when it has become really serious. Get the help of a trusted adult.

✗ Don't stay with a group that forces you to do things. There are lots of other great people out there who would make wonderful friends, if you gave them a chance.

The Outsider

QUIZ

What would you do?

Having a good sense of right and wrong helps you to stay strong under pressure, be true to your values, and make smart choices. Think about how you would respond to pressure in these scenarios. Which is the **most** likely to keep the peace among friends?

TEST TROUBLE

1 The guy next to you turns to you during a test and asks that you show him your answer to a test question. Do you:
a) Tell the teacher immediately?
b) Show him the answer?
c) Ignore him during the test, and tell him later that you didn't want to get yourself or him into trouble?

Drug Thug

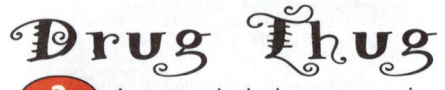

2 A guy at school tries — yet again — to persuade you to buy some dope from him. Do you: a) Give in and buy the dope? b) Punch him out? He won't bother you anymore! c) Tell him that if he bothers you again you'll report it to the teacher or the police?

Class Pass

3 A group of girls is heading off to the mall instead of going to the next class. Do you:
a) Go to the mall with them and hope you don't get caught?
b) Politely bow out and go to the next class?
c) Tell them that if they go you will get them all into trouble?

No Joy

4 A friend wants you to "borrow" a bike for a joyride. Do you:
a) Explain to your friend that you could both get into trouble for stealing?
b) Go for it? Nobody will know who took the bike.
c) Tell your friend's parents, and really get him in trouble?

PARENT PROBLEMS

5 A friend wants you to run away with her because she just had a horrible fight with her parents. Do you:
a) Tell her that running away won't help, and offer to put her up at your place for the night if she lets her parents know where she is?
b) Keep your friend out of trouble by going with her?
c) Tell her that she is a real baby and to quit complaining?

BULLY BOYS

6 A group of guys wants you to go to the neighbourhood park and beat up a kid with them. Do you:
a) Feel a bit uncomfortable about doing this, but go anyway?
b) Tell them that they are all a bunch of goons and you don't want anything to do with them?
c) Tell them you have to be somewhere else? Once you are away from them, report the plan to a trusted adult.

Bum Steer

7 A friend wants you to ride around in a car with her, but she doesn't have a license. Do you:
a) Think "Hey, why not? Nobody will find out."
b) Refuse, and tell her that driving without a license is against the law?
c) Go directly to her parents and let them know what she's been up to?

NEW GUY BLUES

8 The new guy at school invites you to a party. Once you are there, you notice that he and all your friends are drinking. The guy offers you a beer. Do you:
a) Say "no," and have a great time sober? After the party, tell the guy that you don't drink — for future reference.
b) Take the beer and try it?
c) Make a real scene by accusing the guy of trying to get you drunk.

STICKY FINGERS

9 Your friend wants you to shoplift a sweater with her. Do you:
a) Try to persuade her to pay for the sweater?
b) Go straight to store security and tell them that you have a shoplifter for them?
c) Decide that the sweater would really look fabulous with your new jeans.

Date Dilemma

10 You are on the third date with a really cute guy and he is insisting that you fool around. Do you:
a) Feel scared but give in to him?
b) Threaten to tell everyone in the school that he hurt you?
c) Tell him that you like him but are not ready for that. If he persists, do whatever you need to do to get away from him and get help if you need it?

Answers
1. c 2. c 3. b 4. a 5. a 6. c 7. b 8. a 9. a 10. c

The Outsider

There are some basic things to do if you feel you are being pressured

to do something you don't want to do. The first step is to decide exactly what you want for yourself. Then you have to be brave enough to take the steps towards getting it.

Make Up Your Mind
Ask yourself:
- Is it against the rules or my beliefs?
- Is it harmful to others?
- Would it disappoint my family or other people who are important to me?
- Is it wrong?
- Would I be sorry afterward?
- Would I be hurt or upset if someone did this to me?

If you answer "yes" to any of these questions, then you need to say "no" to doing whatever people are trying to get you to do.

Stay Away
Try to avoid the problem in the first place:
- Don't hang out with people who are trying to pressure you.
- Make an excuse and leave.
- Choose your friends wisely. If you stick with people who share your values, you'll probably never be asked to do something you don't want to do.
- If your friends keep bugging you about something and you have tried other strategies, then simply refuse to talk about it. They'll get the message.

Say No
Once you've decided to say no:
- Be firm about it.
- Act confidently when you talk so that people can see you are serious.
- If you can, make a joke to ease the tension, but without putting anyone down. For example, if you are offered a cigarette you could say, " No thanks, my breath is bad enough!"

DID YOU KNOW?

- Teens whose peers are often in trouble with the law commit more than 5 violent acts in a year.

DEAR DR. SHRINK-WRAPPED...

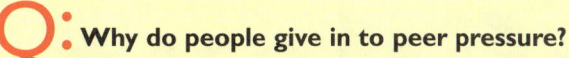

Q: Why do people give in to peer pressure?
— *Bewildered*

A: Dr. Shrink-Wrapped thinks there are many reasons why people give in to peer pressure. Some do it because they are curious to try something new. Others do it because they want to be liked, because they want to fit in, or because they worry that kids will make fun of them if they don't give in to the group.

Q: I have a really tight group of friends. If we all agree to do something or not do something, is that peer pressure?
— *Gal Pals*

A: Not if you all agree! If you choose friends who feel the same as you do about things, you can help each other resist pressure from outside your group. But if one person in the group — say, you — disagrees, and the others try to pressure you, that's a different story. Pressure from friends can be the hardest to deal with. Try these three steps for resisting pressure from friends:
1) Figure out what it is your friends want you to do and how you feel about it. If you are feeling uncomfortable about it, then the odds are you don't really want to do it. 2) Ask yourself what your options are. For each option, ask yourself: Is it safe? Is it fair? Will it work? Will it make everyone feel better? 3) Choose one option and suggest it. If it doesn't work, then try again. If they're really your friends, they're worth the effort to find a solution.

Talk It Out

If you're still getting pressure from friends:
- Explain why you are worried about getting into trouble, getting hurt, or hurting someone else.
- Find an alternative that everyone feels comfortable doing.
- Talk to a teacher, parent, or guidance counsellor you trust. Don't feel guilty if you have made some mistakes. It's better to get help now before the situation gets worse.

- Many teens think all their peers are having sex, but only half of Canadian teens have had sex by age 18.
- Many schools require uniforms so students won't feel pressure to wear "cool" clothes.

The **Witness**

So you are a confident, independent person

who just doesn't do peer pressure — you don't give it and you don't take it. Lucky you! So what do you do when you see it happening to someone else, like a friend? You wouldn't just let it happen…

Would you?

do's and don'ts

✓ Do come to the defense of someone being pressured.

✓ Do let him/her know that you are there to be a friend and not to judge them.
✓ Do let him/her know that he/she has choices in this situation.
✓ Do talk to your friend about the issue, and be a good listener.
✓ Do help your friend make a wise decision.

✓ Do help your friends go through the steps of resisting peer pressure from page 24.
✓ Do tell your friend that if he/she feels pressured again he/she should report it to a trusted adult, like a teacher or parent.

✓ Do tell your friend that, if it is a dangerous or illegal issue, a call to the police may be necessary.

✓ Do encourage a friend to make new friends if his/her current friends seem to be a negative influence.

✗ Don't be critical or judgmental of your friend. Your friend needs your trust and support.
✗ Don't copy the ones putting pressure on your friend by trying to pressure your friend into anything.
✗ Don't let your friend feel as if he/she is alone in the situation.
✗ Don't project your own feelings about the situation onto your friend. Remember to really listen to find out what your friend's feelings and needs are.

The Witness

QUIZ

Do you really get it?

So you think that you know what to do if you see someone being sucked into a group's pressure. But do you really get it? What would you do in the following situations? This quiz has no right or wrong answers, because each situation is unique. Your answers may be different from the ones given below, but they could be right under the circumstances.

DANGER AHEAD

2 Your friend tells you that he is seriously considering joining a gang in his neighbourhood.

- Listen carefully to his reasons for wanting to do it.
- Discuss the risks of gang involvement from p. 19 of this book.
- Help him with strategies for saying "no" to this gang.

GOING TOO FAR?

1 Your best friend tells you that she has been seeing a guy who is pressuring her to have sex, and she feels really confused. This guy wants to see her this evening.

- Listen to your friend and try to help her sort out her feelings.
- Suggest strategies for dealing with this guy, from polite ways of saying "no" to more serious scenarios where she needs to run for safety.
- Ask her if she can call him before tonight's date and tell him how she is feeling.
- Tell her that if she feels confused or uncomfortable, then that means that she needs to think about it before deciding to have sex.

Clothes War

3 You are with a group of girls, and they start making fun of the way another girl is dressed.

- Walk away and don't be part of the teasing.
- Defend the other girl.
- Together with the girl, think up strategies for dealing with the group.

Permanent Problem

4 Your friend tells you that her group is pressuring her to get a huge tattoo of her boyfriend's name on her arm.

- Remind her that tattoos are permanent and she will not be able to erase her boyfriend's name once it's on her arm.
- Discuss the risks of getting tattoos: the chance of infection, getting in trouble with her parents, getting tired of it, etc.
- Suggest she try a temporary tattoo that can be washed off.

Model Image

5 Your best friend tells you she wants to look like her favourite magazine models, who are all beautiful and thin. She has heard that she can lose weight more easily if she throws up her meals, and has started doing that.

- Discuss the fact that most magazine models are airbrushed to look impossibly beautiful.
- Tell her that she already looks fine the way she is.
- Tell her that throwing up her food could lead to an eating disorder.
- If she really wants to lose weight, suggest safer ways, such as exercising or seeing a dietitian.

Continues...

The Witness

QUIZ ... continued

BIG TROUBLE

6 You find out that your friend has started taking steroids because he wants to look athletic like the other guys. He says that everyone is taking them.

- Tell him that he may think that everyone is taking them, but in fact it may be only a few kids in the school.
- Tell him about the dangers of taking steroids.
- Suggest other ways to feel more fit and athletic, like working out with a coach or following a strength-training program from a book.

MISSING IN ACTION

7 Your girlfriend is always ditching school to hang out with her friends. Her marks have already plummeted.

- Remind her that she needs to keep her marks up in order to get into university.
- Ask her why she keeps doing this. Listen carefully to her reasons.
- Suggest ways she could resist pressure from her friends to cut class.

SMOKE CHOKE

8 You are shocked when your friend takes out a cigarette and lights up along with some other pals. He says that you're making too big a deal of it.

- Explain why you don't smoke: the risks of lung cancer and addiction, that other people find it offensive, you/parents would be upset, etc.
- Ask him if he's just trying to feel cool and fit in with his group. Suggest ways to resist that pressure.
- Help him find ways to quit his habit if he has trouble stopping.

E-Rumours

9 A group has turned on your friend and is spreading nasty rumours about her. The leader of the group is asking you to stop being her friend, too.

- Explain to the group that you can make your own decisions about who you will be friends with.
- Tell them that you refuse to hear lies about your friend.
- Tell your friend that the group is spreading rumours about her and together think up ways to deal with the situation.

SCARED STIFF

10 A friend comes to you and tells you that a group of guys called him a fag and wants to beat him up after school. He is really upset and scared.

- Let him know that the school has strict policies about this sort of harassment. If he reports it to the teacher or principal, they will protect him.
- If he is afraid to report, offer to go with him to the teacher for moral support.
- Suggest he tell his parents, so that they can call the police if needed.

More Help

It takes time and practice to learn the skills in this book. There are many ways to deal with peer pressure, but only you know which feels right in each situation. In the end, the best response is the one that keeps you safe.

If you need more help, or someone to talk to, the following resources may be of use.

Helplines and Organizations
Kids Help Phone (Canada)   1-800-668-6868
Youth Crisis Hotline (USA)   1-800-448-4663

Web sites
AADAC Youth Services: www.Zoot2.com
Deal.org
Health Canada – Just for You (Youth) http://www.hc-sc.gc.ca/english/for_you/youth.html
Kids Help Phone: http://kidshelp.sympatico.ca
Lesbian, Gay, Bi Youthline: www.youthline.ca
Media-awareness.ca
National Eating Disorders Centre: www.nedic.ca
Red Cross Interactive Info for Youth: www.redcross.ca
Sexualityandu.ca
Stay Alert… Stay Safe: www.sass.ca
Your Life: Your Choice!: www.schoolnet.ca/alcohol/
Youthpath.ca

Books
After Dinner Barf by A.D. Fast. Vanwell Publishing, 2002.
Bat Summer by Sarah Withrow. Groundwood Books, 1998.
The Complete Idiot's Guide To Peer Pressure for Teens by Hilary Cherniss and Sara Jane Sluke, Alpha Books, 2001.
Corner Kick by Bill Swan. James Lorimer & Company, 2004.
Courage on the Line by Cynthia Bates. James Lorimer & Company, 1999.
Getting a Life by Jocelyn Shipley. Sumach Press, 2002.
Edge by Diane Tullson. Stoddart Kids, 2002.
The Hunger by Marsha Skrypuch. Boardwalk Books, 1999.
Men of Stone by Gayle Friesen. Kids Can Press, 2000.
The Only House by Teresa Toten. Red Deer Press, 1995.
Scarface by Paul Kropp. Hi Interest Publishing, 2002.
Sparks by Graham McNamee. Random House, 2002.
Stitches by Glen Huser. Groundwood Books, 2003.
A Taste of Perfection by Laura Langston. Stoddart Kids, 2002.
Tribes by Arthur Slade. HarperCollins, 2002.
Moonkid and Prometheus by Paul Kropp. Stoddart Kids, 1997.
My Name is Mitch by Shelagh Lynne Supeene. Orca Book Publishers, 2003.
Turns on a Dime by Julie Lawson. Stoddart Kids, 1998.
Walking a Thin Line by Sylvia McNicoll. Scholastic Canada, 1997.

Text copyright © 2004 by Elaine Slavens
Illustrations copyright © 2004 by Ben Shannon

All rights reserved. No part of this book may be reproduced or transmitted in any form or by any means, electronic or mechanical, including photocopying, or by any information storage or retrieval system, without permission in writing from the Publisher.

James Lorimer & Company Ltd. acknowledges the support of the Ontario Arts Council. We acknowledge the support of the Government of Canada through the Book Publishing Industry Development Program (BPIDP) for our publishing activities. We acknowledge the support of the Canada Council for the Arts for our publishing program. We acknowledge the support of the Government of Ontario through the Ontario Media Development Corporation's Ontario Book Initiative.

Design: Blair Kerrigan/Glyphics

National Library of Canada Cataloguing in Publication Data

Slavens, Elaine
  Peer pressure : deal with it without losing your cool / Elaine Slavens.

ISBN 1-55028-815-6

  1. Peer pressure—Juvenile literature. 2. Peer pressure in children—Juvenile literature.
  I. Title.
HQ784.P43S52 2004   j303.3'27   C2004-900477-8

James Lorimer & Company Ltd., Publishers
35 Britain Street
Toronto, Ontario
M5A 1R7
www.lorimer.ca

Distributed in the United States by:
Orca Book Publishers
P.O. Box 468 Custer, WA
USA 98240-0468

Printed and bound in China